INTEN
OR THE WEIGHT O

ROO BORSON

M&S

Canadian Cataloguing in Publication Data

Borson, Roo, 1952-
Intent, or, The weight of the world

Poems.
ISBN 0-7710-1588-7

I. Title. II. Title: The weight of the world.

PS8553.O786I68 1989   C811'.54   C89-093308-1
PR9199.3.B67I68 1989

The publisher would like to thank the Ontario Arts Council for its financial assistance.

Photographs in text by Sue Schenk

Set in Joanna by The Typeworks, Vancouver
Printed and bound in Canada

McClelland & Stewart Inc.
The Canadian Publishers
481 University Avenue
Toronto, Ontario M5G 2E9

They are not "truths," but should be used as phenomenological guides until verified.

—Rajan Gupta,
from the lectures on lattice gauge theories

Certain dreams presage true events.
If a woman, for instance, in mid-life
dreams that from her own body,
attached and tingling, a penis buoys up
with such lust as has followed her all her days,
like a naughty, dangerous puppy,
always at the heels,
and should she dream then from the other side,
not of Lethe between life and death
but of another, unnamed river, then upon waking
her allegiances may be realigned
as utterly as the magnetic poles of the earth.

And should it, the next night, occur
that her lover, overtaken by lust as seldom before, require,
because the small-walled house is bright with invited strangers,
that they step out for a moment where the blackened woods
are tethered all around in the eye of the storm
which has not yet finished with them,
and that her garments be taken down under this new
          government
too about to fall, of stars unevenly revealed in the shaky coup,
then the Seven Sisters, the Pleiades, of whom there are truly
          eight
but the eighth is clairvoyant and sickly,
then the Seven Sisters look down upon this scene and are
          jealous.

And the third thing,
this light in the brain which is like the eighth Sister,
a shimmer, an urge, not to be lost but found, so strong
that the lazily unwilling fingers comply to write this down,
this third thing is like the eighth Sister,

or the persistently dimming flashlight which ceased
– and would always cease –
to shed sufficient light on what they were
doing on their way to the woods.

The first buzz saw,

and suddenly, in sunlight,
everyone has eyelashes.

Doors left open for a breeze
stay open. No breeze,

only the dusty smell of planks, of
lost homework in the gutters,

and all afternoon a swing keeps weeping,
on and on.

So it is that the fruit bowl,
clustered with tiny wings,
seems just about to fly,

and bread stales quickly,
squeaks against the teeth.

All day, because of roads and tunnels,
the immense sound of ball bearings
rolling down an inclined plane,

and there is an old recording,

and a dog barks, come evening,
under the trees.

People rush by. It's a way they have,
but really there isn't any hurry.

Someone carries off the bodies of the dead, without a fuss.
Then it's just the belongings.

Loyalty or necessity, which is it
for the wristwatch marking time on a stranger's arm?

At any moment the gears mesh at only one point,
that's the way it is.

Trains, too, pace the length and breadth of the continent,
the passengers growing more raucous as each destination nears.

In life, each of us starts out with a howl,
a shout from the depths, every failure is a blessing!

The train stops.
Someone leaves, another takes his place.

It's a quiet time, full of bustle and commotion.
The sound of a wristwatch, but no goodbyes.

In Ontario, in autumn,
black and limp, with shining curves,
they are the only footwear for the fields.
All year they have lain in
fishy heaps at the back of closets
and now halls and entryways
are lined with them, pair by pair,
dripping onto newspaper,
upright, leaning drunkenly together, or toppled,
helpless as dull black beetles,
their legs in the air.
I remember the morning
Jane fell in love, in San Francisco,
with a pair,
glazed, brilliant as lemons
in the shop window.
But what shines in a wild Pacific storm
would leak within minutes
when the world turns to mud
and sucks at the heels
in Elora or Owen Sound.
A gash is an unhappy thing,
especially in black rubber,
when boots are cheap:
the kind thing is to carve
the toes like jack-o'-lanterns
and let them leer
unexpectedly in hallways.
Nothing mourns like a boot
for its lost mate.
You must fill it with water,
and flowers.
Unlike other shoes,
they never smell of possession.

They have mapped the sodden marsh,
trod on ice.
You step into them,
sound and seamless,
with a double pair of thick socks.
You enter the Ark.

CHITONS

We found one, one summer,
my aunt and sister and I,
beachcombing for tiny minarets
and sea-ground glass
off Havensneck, dead.

Breathless, empty-headed, still squinting
from continuous wind, as after a long ride
one feels still in motion –
we dumped a mosaic onto the table.
The chiton like a bloated boot sole
washed up from somebody drowned.
Curious, unsure,

we took a kitchen knife
and sliced through
to the sudden organs:
orange and magenta.
With such colours, my sister said,
they had to be for sex,
and whooped once with delight.

Says Webster, *the related but more advanced*
cephalopod
has a depressed body, and the power to eject
a black, ink-like fluid to darken the water
and conceal itself when in danger.
Gumboots, the locals call them,
as opposed to *chiton*,
which leads us back to the ancient Greeks,
who wore a tunic or undergarment of the same name,

so we think of Sappho,
especially in winter, when the tide

7

and the old year are receding.
Then they can be found along the foam line,
where storms bury and unbury them,
big as a baby's foot
or the workboot of a large man –
or at nightfall,
above the tideline,
where they resemble footprints going out to sea,
and fill us with unease.

The shovel's empty mouth,
the rusted lashes of the rake,
the saw aswim on the sunlit worktable.

The oak at the edge of the field
with the lights of home in it,
the flies hooking to the screen before a storm.

Blizzard of summer seeds,
cows that groan through the premature dusk,
leaves falling through the walls.

Even the cat, outside, who leaps
to hang by his claws from the screen,
and follows us this way from room to room.

Miles of approaching rain, the gradual
extinction: abandoned things which once were tame,
and the tame which once were wild, two-faced, fey.

Thinking of the wild grasses of
my childhood hillside,
my father's ashes
mingling with the soil,
I come again upon
the child I was, asleep
between impermeable walls,
who wakens, paralyzed with
terror in the summer night:
two inches of incarnate dread
against the whiteness of the sheet,
that rigid small voice
calling for my father.
Wordless they come to us,
the moth adhering to the mirror's surface,
an albino spider caught in the long
straws of a broom:
cool as grass.
I lie awake and listen
to my own house shift and settle.
A complete world of faucets and switches,
stairways into warmth,
what we think of as safety.
Greetings,
I say,
to the invisible cracks,
the delicate mask-like being that will
pause, and enter.

Last night on our way to the bathroom after making love
the neighbour's house lights must have stolen
a little way through the kitchen window; as we passed,

the two white bentwood chairs I had brought
with me from Vermont and another life
glowed with a faint, ulterior, mineral half-life –

illusion of a snowed-in night without moon in Vermont.
As once, after a convivial late night with friends,
my companion and I stepped out to a world

not as we'd left it; for while we drank and talked,
obliviously, snow had been falling,
and it had grown clear again, and very cold,

so that the ground glowed, risen several inches.
We weren't dressed for it,
yet chose to walk back by way of the woods,

whose paths, muddled of late by too much use,
had been obliterated by snow, so that we sank
deeper at each step, laughing.

Last night on our way back through the kitchen,
after the brightness of the bathroom, our eyes would not adjust;
the chairs had melded with the dark, and we stumbled.

Yet back in bed as I turned toward sleep
the paths became confused again,
my former life drifting across our life:

I was young, half-dreaming,
and because I had no past to speak of I went forward,
into a cold so extreme

it was at the same time exotically warm –
as though there were no way to distinguish
between the pleasure and the ache,

or to choose, last night,
in the after-ache of pleasure,
between my life and my life.

2 A.M., and the clocks have been turned
one hour backwards. Summer's gone,
like rage or pleasure, the
possum we caught rolling,
drunk on garbage,
over the fence one morning,

and now the rain:
a glimpse, sometimes,
as of a second chance –
not fully fallen into sleep,
to be awakened.

up through the field once more.
Sat in impressions where deer have lain.
Broken windowpane. Sungazing.
The town of Gualala,
hidden beyond ripples of forest.
So,
goodbye to berry picking,
visions of plenitude from the station-wagon window,
those singular, wild meals,
the time we stumbled on the site
of the long-burnt-down cabin,
someone that slept through death,
and oh those yellow plums sweetened on disaster,
the looks between us then,
goodbye to memory.
                              And yet much
stays with us. That
August is for huckleberries,
where the best apples are, that delicate
complete skeletons are to be found in the winter rain.
The back left leg of the woodstove, though,
must be propped with stones,
the well water turns bourbon purple.
It hardly matters, you'd say,
indoors or out,
one never has to *dress* here.
The light of a reading lamp,
and I a wall away, under the meteor shower,
my flesh of your flesh,
each rare event plotted and erased.
To think *never again* or *friendless*,
to think *my mother's cool hands*,

and, like a secret, the earth orchids
year after year that come
up again under the redwoods,
but they won't find you.

Rain hitting the shovel
leaned against the house,
rain eating the edges
of the metal in tiny bites,
bloating the handle,
cracking it.
The rain quits and starts again.

There are people who go into that room in the house
where the piano is and close the door.
They play to get at that thing
on the tip of the tongue,
the thing they think of first and never say.
They would leave it out in the rain if they could.

The heart is a shovel leaning against a house somewhere
among the other forgotten tools.
The heart, it's always digging up old ground,
always wanting to give things a decent burial.

But so much stays fugitive,
inside,
where it can't be reached.

The piano is a way of practising
speech when you have no mouth.
When the heart is a shovel that would bury itself.
Still we can go up casually to a piano
and sit down and start playing
the way the rain felt in someone else's bones
a hundred years ago,
before we were born,
before we were even one cell,
when the world was clean,

when there were no hearts or people,
the way it sounded
a billion years ago, pattering
into unknown ground. Rain

hitting the shovel leaned against the house,
eating the edges of the metal.
It quits,
        and starts again.

Along Bloor, toward one end of the Annex or another,
or up Yonge, half-eclipsed already,
or Kensington before a storm –
in all kinds of weather, it seemed, we kept walking toward
        dinner,
bouquets for friendship, a bottle to unlock the night,
to report, while our lives stood still,
the snubs, infatuations, gossip
we called it
but really it was our common life.

A storm coming, and in the leaves
a tickling, choking music. To sit in comfort as the
last dumb souls doubletake and run for cover,
and lightning
lights the rain.
Susan, in love, could make an orange last an hour,
dreamily deliberate. Midnight on the telephone
any one of us might need to be talked down into sleep.
And if we paired off from time to time wasn't it partly
for the flush feeling of coming back to the others again?
– more alive, privileged, at one with the city.
Or stepping out of a bar, late,
the first flakes in our faces;
an overcast that would stall for days, while down Bay
scraps shot the windy rapids.
The night we skated the icy sidewalks in our shoes!
Slid along arm in arm, interchangeable, tangled.
And then, all at once, summer.

Ten P.M., humidity one hundred percent.
A boy swerving in figure eights on a bicycle
calling out to the woman passing,
surrounding her in himself-and-bicycle.

The trees voluminous, lit from within.
We'd sit out late on Nathan's porch,
the brief, suggestive breezes,
wild kittens climbing up for milk,
a saucer beside the door,
while their mother Blackie, shier
than each of her successive broods,
twined and twined amid the morning glories.
Beyond the rooftops, the crosshatched power lines,
that uncanny everlasting blue.
Leaning back, staring up, immersed,
we'd feel the undertow begin to pull,
that some of us would move on,
the circle be broken. But on such nights
no – though we'd disperse then,
tired but not sleepy,
on the casual wafting dark. Stared at
from the trees – raccoon –
just long enough to identify.
Things there and not there.
And so to bed, wide-eyed in the dark.

The places we inhabited are gone. The restaurants,
kitchens, those fatal bedrooms. Bryan's Caesar salads.
Carolyn's treacherous secrets. And what remains
is a primitive mnemonic of smells and tastes – mock
competitions, old loves, caramelized pears
on a white platter. Those tricky streets,
the one-way maze, long nights of talking.
Windows we glance into.
There and not there.
Along Sullivan, Lowther, Borden.

Lying back, listening to my arm hurt. First hesitating notes of rain, and across the city an infant erupting out of sleep into crying, one natural motion, a bird flushed from foliage, crying not for any outer reason, just following the brain's score as it's written. Lying flat, listening to the pain in my arm. A pastorale this time, old arguments beaten out in the rainfall, that familiar cadence. How I would at this moment be lying three thousand miles from myself had I not been distracted a dozen times from an obvious future. And now the gentle nudge in my arm pretending to be a clock that will always keep good time: as well to believe in a way of making choices. Throb of hoofbeats in damp ground, little aches, the hard rain that ruins nothing, few are out in the rain that don't want to be, out in the waltzing storm. Afterwards, from roofs, treetops, the dwindling drops, echoing and harmless as those last unaimed shots fired in homesickness, just before cease-fire. It's a new form of the blues the leftover rain picks out, twice-fallen. The kind you play in the dark, after everyone's been sung down into sleep with whatever it was they needed to hear.

We're out with the night beings,
pale airborne zig-zags,
the staggered race through headlights,
once or twice a coyote,
the colour of straw, as ragged,
beings that cross us always from left to right,
barely missed by windshield or tires,
identified by stripe or snout or size
or not at all.
It was in Truth Or Consequences, New Mexico
we tried to stop,
after a rained-out rodeo, local festivities.
Finally found a room, though there was trouble
with a missing key. Unlocked the door to a boy
sitting up suddenly drunk in the dark
on a bed we had bought for the night.
He's not the kind to hurt you, said the desk clerk,
who was also a mother and mistress to a small silent dog
in a rhinestone collar, from behind a display
of earrings on a dead cholla branch,
and anyway he's gone.
We were tired, but took our money and moved on,
because we could,
not sentenced to that town,
we thought, as the boy was, probably for life.
We moved on
with the night beings from the other world,
which is also our world,
with speed and inattention,
one of those beautiful emptying hand puppets
now and then by the roadside,
"Guernica," as Klee might have painted it, for a windshield,
through desert where motels grow
arid and square with names like The Sands and Oasis.

At certain points in the universe longing condenses,
the shade sucked against the screen,
the plain dishevelled ruffles that frame
the window – because a girl sleeps here during
the year, a school, a desk, the simple chair whose
duty and forgiveness are the weight of all matter.
A month from now someone's daughter
will enter this room,
her hair will fall along her back,
she will sit in struggle with
thoughts not her own, the books in front of her,
hour after hour – medieval really,
this illimitable patience, as at the bedside
of the dying, whom one loves –
and how the skin and breasts are lit by faint
sensations, that which asks as well
for knowledge through another.
What can be discovered within four walls?
Walls a pale green found nowhere in
nature but in the wings of a rare
moth that startled me once,
near, as big as my hand,
and whose coloration
mimics it.
Let us call it
learning, redisposing oneself, hour after hour,
to be as one is urged, cajoled,
told. I have lived in this room,
made love here, the man sleeps beside me.
Will she sense our trespass as an opening?
Or will she, like the local girl who served our dinner,
a few dollars and a summer job with which to

dabble in freedom,
think this town ugly,
because that is how she sees her life so far,
and she has not lived elsewhere.

Hiked for three days
in the fierce warm wind.
Saw lightning,
black butterflies,
burning blue wildflowers,
cow chimes.
Saw a cave
where a prehistoric stream had carved
the initial outline,
a spotted horse,
saw the handprint.

Couldn't sleep
for what I had seen.

Nothing prepares us for it,
no memorizing of lists, numbers,
past events – no geometrician,
chemist, cubist, farmer
can subtract a hairsbreadth
from our ignorance.
Astronomy is mute,
economics and the law are mute (not to mention
the plumber, the butcher, the gardener).
In the face of it theology is a padded room;
there is no study, whim, invention,
no field of enquiry – and, once there,
no addendum, no redress,
no bargain struck with god,
no god.
And this first step, misguided, careless,
finding one must begin again! – this first step
makes us ache to go on from there –
but there are no more steps to be taken,
no legs, or hands, or feet,
no walls,
no shoes.

All day, lonely for my childhood, I've been picking up apples and tossing them down again. Rotten. The birches, the maples have lowered their red and yellow flags to half-mast, and now and then a bird rises up into the sky, the blackened silhouette of a hand-drawn angel.

Here is autumn. Though I know you've seen autumn for yourself, take it. I've wrapped it in a little of all that surrounds us, hoping you won't notice right away there can be nothing inside, nothing to claim or give.

Knowing you know this.

Now and then, like someone tuning a harp, the isolated sprinkle of rain against the cabin window.

One night goes on longer than the rest, never so long,
whiled away. Then dawn.
Goodbye, insects. Hollow casings on the windowsill,
a dainty leg among the spice jars.
Goodbye, marigolds, the earth will not wait for you.
Trains hurtle by at the edges of cities,
the taste of bourbon, a mouthful of leaves.
Above everyone's dining-table a chandelier burns.
Now the luxurious old wine can be uncorked,
the slicing of meat and bread, uncorked,
and in the black panes life goes on.

THE MERCHANTS' SONG

after "Foxfire" by Hiroshige

Through the night-blue fields, with lanterns, we go,
under the leafless ayenoki,
and the ghostly foxes
shelter under dry branches and unwinking stars.
Toward the distant houses of Oji,
toward the slopes coated with pine
we make our way,
and we with our lanterns are
flames in air, the burning aether.
We come to collect the unpaid bills,
for the new year is upon us,
and those not paid this last night of December
must wait until April.
Here, in the cropped fields of Oji,
among encampments of foxes,
their slender ears and ankles,
the stooks which stand like silent peasants,
we take our rest,
for there are those among us
who have died this year,
and must wander tonight, forever,
unseen, except as flame among the foxes,
collecting bills which will not be paid
in April, or ever.

I cry for my father because of everyone's short sleeves.
Because of legs and the solemn, thoughtless act of walking.
Because shops are full of goods and they keep ordering more.
Because there is a new kind of metal,
and ties still hang in closets,
and it is Tuesday.
Because of the existence of books,
of boxer shorts, and fedoras, and baseball season,
which will begin again.
Because "dust" is a euphemism
and "cremains" is a new noun
that wasn't in the old dictionary,
because they fit into a gold box the size of a Steuben sculpture.
Because "ashes" is a euphemism
and the box is unexpectedly heavy
and California is flooded
and the fragments are in the rain.
Because bone is variously tubular and spongy
and glows in the dark.
Because it is edible and can be read by.
Because it is possible to throw away someone's false teeth
but not their glasses.

To go about in public.
To pass by pastry shops and galleries.
To curse the feet for knowing how to walk,
the skin which keeps on feeling,
and the eyes, to curse them too.
But no one goes blind,
no buildings burn,
the body keeps turning vegetables and meat
into urine and hair.
How unsuspectingly the clothes go on without us,
airy, startled scarecrows.
To walk the firm earth then,
on hard leather soles, upright.
But there is a place we may lie down.
Amid the weightless silence of public spaces.

You needn't search for it, in your searching.

PINE

Pine, asleep in the sunshine,
I think I'll lie down near you and sleep awhile.

I've been hard-headed of late, surprised by an empty heart.
Tired of everything I know.

I went walking through one of the winding,
wealthier districts. High up,
inside one of the houses: someone practising scales.
A fading, ordered loneliness as the houses gave way
to woods, the sidewalk became a path, and farther on,
a hunched shape, unmoving, as in grief or worse,
resolved in silence as I neared
into two – taken up entirely – and a pair of glasses,
lain aside no doubt for intimacy,
through which, as I stepped around them,
the forest floor appeared, magnified.
Where I'd seen that shape before I couldn't say,
a late-night thriller maybe, the single figure
hunched over the transmitter, tapping, again and again,
the fingers on the keys. This is what came back to me,
how clear it was, the signature of touch,
the need to be believed. I made my way then, down
and down toward the warmth of stalled traffic,
the lowland of the city. Day had lapsed almost into dusk.
Whole streets were lighting up suddenly below me.

The leaves band together and go eddying, skirting the ground, an inch above it, riding invisible paths and invisible Ferris wheels, they go scuffling down roads, whirling into fields. Across the hill-sides the new bales, evenly spaced, give off a bodily heat. Leather fields of turned clay, like acres of hooves. Those two horses we see sometimes, running in the fields, those two who pressed their faces like long solemn loaves against the trailer window in the middle of the night – they frightened us half to death! With their firm bewildered freeness, they knew how to explore: they shamed us by merely looking in. How stiff we lay in our bed, clutching each other. While they, escaped and free, went trotting together along roads laid out by their strange benefactors, we who spare the apple trees their lives in the fenced fields, the last apples like painted wood with soft, striated brushstrokes. Those two horses pass us by with the scenery; they have each other.

Overnight everything has whitened in the web of first frost and suddenly the first travelling flakes are dizzying the air. The oil heater shudders on and off, making little dungeon-sounds, and down the length of the trailer the fridge hisses and trembles, propelling itself through time. Those horses appear again in the yard, their dirty cotton manes torn by burrs and seeds. Pawing the ground as if they didn't remember...having simply lost whatever wild earth smell they were following. They sniff the last of our garden, the toothless cobs on their dried stalks. One of them, taking the lead, swivels his beautiful body, but they do not look back at us. We who built the orchards and the roads.

Waking, it is spring, and these are the birds, the sound of glass shattering at the approach of something infinitely piercing, beyond human range.

Each year the breezes come, carrying contagion, blowing into our heads a fine carelessness, making our bodies light and willing until we're not ourselves anymore, happy to dispense with all we've worked for...and the disease lets us believe we can live this way, we'd rather die of it than go back.

By evening only one bird is left singing, the one we've grown used to, night after night on the same branch. Sweet and irritable, as if called back from sleep. Taking up my glass, rounding the rim with a wetted finger, I can set it ringing – the clear outlines of branch and bud, sky and ground, still bare to the eye.

Between freckles, where the hands become transparent,
there are strange valleys, ashen rivers,
wounds that no longer heal.
One pore on the right cheek
filling with dirt for years.
But the toenails
are horn, are curved. Clearly they are
animal, and of the forests –
of the deserts of our origin.

We find our way back, she and I,
to childhood and summer.
Two generations.
I know the streets, but she knows the lie of the land.
Hills and sea, not far the river,
and the Mission, of another time –
the worn tile, dripping eaves, the garden
where the good Father strolled with his god.
And how his ghost stares openly from objects:
frugal bed, the robe beside it,
plates set for the tardy traveller.
It doesn't change much, land.
Someone comes, someone goes.
Soon what lies ahead lies behind.
We find our way back, she and I.
To rest our feet awhile
in the fine, hot sand. And not a word.
The white, white sand where lost spoons lie.

The other week in a department store
I picked up a pair of shoes from a clearance table
and couldn't tell
whether they were ugly or beautiful.
Stricken by this
inability to *see*,
and all the hands groping around me,
I spent the rest of the day
wandering from store to store.

Nonetheless it was the first day I could see
a way out of winter –
buds silhouetted along branches overhead –
and I remarked to several people
how warm it was,
the first spring-like day of the year.
A woman who worked in a bookstore
said she'd had to run back from lunch
it had been so cold.
Still, the clouds wore a soft blossoming look.
Later, a freezing wind.

On friends' recommendations
I'd been going from book to book,
movie to movie,
different prescriptions
but no cure.

It had been like gradually
losing the use of an arm,
like a piece of equipment that isn't working,
when everything looks okay on the outside,
so the problem must be farther in.

Someone I knew
had been depressed for several years,
told me the story of how
one day he was playing tennis,
and all at once,
seemingly in one thwack of the ball,
back up through the arm,
sensation rushed into him.

All around me people passed
with tightened lips, concentrating hard.
The two parrots that lived upstairs
conversed in unrelated syllables,
chains of abusive, deficient,
mutant English –

Went to the zoo,
and while my friends were watching the gorillas
I couldn't take my eyes from the kids,
snorting, scratching their armpits,
aping cartoons.

I wanted to
hold my mind up next to other minds;

I remembered all the unfinished projects
grudgingly;

things that passed between people,
a look,
a breeze of understanding,

like exotic delicacies
from paradise –

It had been like boarding a jetliner
for a destination far from waking life.

At first my dreams were lush, tinged sometimes
with a morbid eroticism,
morally timid –

In the morning I would pluck
clinging hairs from the pillow;
for hours the afterglow of dreaming would accompany me.
In my encounters
I could have been a mere silhouette, backlit
by this radiance
that gradually decayed . . .

Trying to settle down with a book,
after a few sentences I'd feel put out;
I'd pick things up, a letter, a bookmark,
and simply let them drop . . .

Still, all things considered,
I felt "fine,"
just as when you answer the telephone
and, instead of the dreaded, anticipated voice,
it's a friend, whom you like – relieved,
you do suddenly feel "fine" –

Conversation was like that,
trying to pass someone coming toward you down an aisle,
who's trying to pass someone coming toward them down an
        aisle –

More and more I wanted to sleep,
but there were too many items on the agenda,
jumbled, troubling vectors of thought –

And then I did not dream at all.

Eventually I must have been captured, carried off
by sleep
but without dreams, sensations, or consent.
Sleep like a kind of vegetable amnesia.
And though it *happened* to me,
I could not *experience* it.

I was reminded of an old friend
whose comment on the last few years was
"I'd go to the movies
and out of all the people in the theatre
I was the only one laughing."

Meanwhile everything worked normally,
supermarkets remained open,
electricity surged on command...

At an outdoor wedding
I desperately needed to
sneak a laugh.
I didn't dare
turn toward my companion;
glancing sideways I could tell
he too was avoiding contact,
the moment when we would
disgrace ourselves with laughter,
and the other guests
all standing entranced on the lawn...

I was so far inside myself.
Hours would pass, waiting to be lifted out of it;

I'd go to the window and back again,
or stumble over the cat.
I was *sorry* about everything.

Someone would ask for a match
and without thinking I'd give them a lecture.

Squirrels, in the live
foreign world, raced through the trees.

Whenever I forced myself to dress up
I could see that I was "pretty."
"Pretty," but stiff.
And if, by accident,
my thighs brushed together,
I was repulsed –

More and more what stood out
were not people's looks or gestures
but what propped them up,

the grandiose belief in a saviour,

the assumption,
dumb, unyielding, vapid,
that everything is *caused*...

A man and a woman on a sidewalk, for example,
who've been introduced once or twice
and haven't quite sorted out each other's names:
even if they've met by chance,

immediately,
as though it had been planned,
their conversation angles
toward camouflaged probing;
bluffing a little, to show control
but also interest –

There must have been inklings, glimpses –

I could tell I was intentionally
overlooking evidence.

And then, one evening,
in a restaurant with live opera,
the performers were able to hold their smiles
even through strenuous arias.
Between acts I went up to compliment the singers,
who only glanced back distractedly, barely polite –
for an instant the discrepancy might have hurt me,
but afterwards I felt proud of myself,
and of them.
Their earlier look of delight
had been so moving:
such delight *existed*.

It was afternoon already,
after the hard rains.
We were watching the sun go down,
clouds outlined in red neon,
as my friend began abruptly, open-endedly, to laugh.
Laughter like a revolving door,
glee, irony, forgiveness –

And though I had not expected it,
had not willed it,
here and there along the branches,
pink blossoms had broken out

Open the door on spring.
Wildflowers and spiders.
A few bones,
chalky and angular,
dug up by the rain.
Little puzzle of mortality.
A spadeful of earth
with the sun on it.
One shard.
One marble.
Most of a life.

One day a year,
unmarked on any calendar,
not necessarily the same
from valley to valley
or year to year,
it comes. Wafting.
A little warmth to the joints,
and sweaters and jackets wrap their arms
around the waists of pedestrians,
trees lean wistfully over paths,
and sunlight – sunlight everywhere,
like transubstantiated butter.
In college towns fraternities advertise
Spring Bash!
Free Beer For Co-eds!
Passengers lean from speeding windows,
the postman makes his rounds earlier than usual,
peanut butter and jelly sandwiches
taste good again, for a day,
the dead stay dead,
and in the branches, Spring –
: mute tremolo of fingers
: dashes hats off heads
: goes around lifting skirts
: ferries the clouds.

ROBERT PINSKY WAS STANDING ON THE CORNER IN A BLACK
LEATHER JACKET WITH HIS FACE SCREWED UP INTO A MOUE

I dreamed I was reading some new poems by Robert Pinsky,
beautiful poems, the first ending with an off-rhyme on *life* or *lie*,
the second called "Deep Structure Of The Boy And Girl,"
whose title I had just been struck by,
when I awoke, cheated of the poem,
on this chilly March day, in a flurry of blossoms,
wishing, briefly, to be living in another age.

He goes travelling on business and, all at once, reaching into a cupboard or stooping for a crumb, I notice myself. Still, there are simple tasks: sew on the missing buttons, find a movie on TV – anything! – well, almost anything – eat. Seemingly insurmountable blocks of time can be whittled away like this, piecemeal, with nothing but a small fingernail file. Like Miyoshi, then, one buys a red apple, a present to oneself; tries on all the rarely worn but beautiful clothes; fashions complicated hairdos held in place only by the fingers. Imagine the blonde curls and tight linen suits! And his return, then. What, to him, is fixed, what he loves, from a distance – how frangible it is, the thighs and cuticles, the mysteries of the hairline. To study one's body, then, in great detail, memorizing it. And one can always shout out – with little hope, it's true, of being heard – *Farewell! Farewell!* to the small unruly clouds in their solemn pilgrimmage.

Where his hand glides my body turns,
not to pearl, but to a tough, soft being
that would live in mother-of-pearl.

Where his eyes rest,
and there is time,
we are a raft and a rider, adrift.

FINGERNAILS

There are women with fingernails of glass,
at the merest dalliance of whose hands
objects are transported, visibly, from
here to there, as if blessed with precise edges.
In their presence
cool summer drinks effervesce, and men
in white linen suits from all around
traverse the green expanse of August,
like moths toward a lamp at twilight.

I, on the other hand, am fascinated,
have always been
gifted with a visionary clumsiness,
never knowing where the world stops and I begin.

As for my fingernails, sometimes I think
they are more like the acute
growing horns of small animals, tiny
and fierce.

Dog shit
orbited by flies a
beetle
shunning the pebbly
divide all things cross
or else stay
clear to either side
a lizard
pausing in
plastic armour the
infinitely
disintegrating clouds
all things
bright with being
in the sunstruck
hills where a
plane just now
grazes us with shadow
spits us out.
Birds in scrambled
song networks
of berryvine
cow parsnip
purslane
the
intimate disinterest
by which all
things are held
in the one
stretched
open-ended moment –
and the rest is
memory
and

though the up-and-down
jogs it free
doesn't bear repeating.
Bear grass.
Oat grass.
Blackberry.
Blackberry.

To board the train for Toronto and glance over at the other
track as that train starts rolling and the woman there,
opposite, dozing, opens her eyes.
To look into eyes and know there are many directions.
To have it all at once: cinnamon buns
from the Harbord Bakery and the late poems of Wang Wei.
To step out, bringing traffic to a halt.
To bemoan with total strangers the state of the lettuce,
to be queried concerning the uses of star fruit,
and expostulate thereon.
To guide an unsteady gentleman across the street
and refuse payment in eternity.
To happen on the long light down certain streets as the sun is
        setting,
to pass by all that tempts others without a thought.
For cigar smoke and Sony Walkmans and random belligerence,
the overall sense of delighted industry
which is composed of idle hatred, inane self-interest,
compassion, and helplessness, when looked at closely.
To wait in queues, anonymous as the price code in a
        supermarket.
To board a bus where everyone is talking at once,
and count eight distinct languages, and not know any.
For the Chinese proprietress of the Bagel Paradise Restaurant,
who is known to her customers as the joyful
otter is known to the clear salt water of Monterey Bay.
To know that everyone who isn't reading, daydreaming,
or on a first date is either full of plans or
playing Sherlock Holmes on the subway.
For eerie cloudlit nights, and skyscrapers,
and raccoons, jolly as bees.
For the joy of walking out the front door and becoming
instantly, and resolutely, lost.

To fall, when one is falling,
into a safety net, and find one's friends.
To be one among many.
To be many.

Swallows diving and sweeping, high voltage wires stringing it all together, the chirring restlessness and drifting, dreaming plants. No wind. Just vines gone astray, green and red berries strung along them. And in the field a half-fallen house keeps silence inside it, uncertain place, its missing roof that might have held a cross or a bell, white fluttering paint, and at the underedges, perpetually cool, tongues of fungi attach themselves; spiders that move slantwise with the controlled breadth of a pianist's hands over abandoned mason jars. Day in, year out, the inadvertent lighting of these lamps that aren't lamps, for the return of what won't return. A snail flows gracefully through the grass, a ship riding the wavelets of its own rippling flesh, but so slowly, it might as well be the broken ornamental head of a fallen column.

In the blue light at the far end of the darkened house,
shadowy players shoot and score,
continual apocalypse in the announcer's voice.
My companion, lost to it,
dark negative of the self,
one silhouetted foot jutting into the near light of the TV.
Distanced roar of speed and heroics,
the miniaturized raging and cheering.
Now and then against the quiet of the house
his wild dissension, little world,
and the cat moves like a lament,
its wants not the usual ones,
not usual and so
indefinite, unmet.

Sand or snow?
Snow, I think, despite
the coarse foreground grass,
as in a child's
version of earth,
for there are
grey hoofprints –
the horse
here canters
knowingly, for sport,
hoofs raised.
In watercolour, as in dreams,
several things
are true at once.
The horse, unevenly illumined,
in candlelight beside the evening meal,
runs blinkered,
though there is no sign
of harness, horse
that's never saddled,
and the same dark stroke in daylight
is the body's structure.
Not simultaneous, then,
but as in dreams,
where the shifts are not of time,
but of what we take
to be there, because we see it.
A horizon where trees blur.
And distance.
The horse's speed.
How, suddenly, it lies
beyond the frame,
the longer view,
and lost to us.

Small perfumed pears grow here,
numerous and hidden as birds' eggs in June.
Small perfumed pears, and half-wild plums.
I'm as far as ever from what I love.
All day masses of cloud drifting south
approach the pine tree and move on,
a mile high, to other places.

A moment of silence, then,
for the old-fashioned beauty parlour,
for the barber pole,
and the corner grocery,
a moment for the peeling billboards
and the smiling vagrant dogs,
the silenced taps
in the drugstore soda fountain,
a moment of silence
for a kind of trust,
for what we think of
as the world,
each generation,
as we're born to it,
those rare boulevards of leafy trees,
the last straight roads with life on them,
and architecture,
and a golden age of beards
still to be found on men drinking
beer from glasses, of a life
for silverware and plates and cafés –
the sudden homesickness
for an age,
long past midday or toward evening,
to be able to cross
from the shade to the
sunny side, and tall blooms
cup the sunlight,
the desire to stand forever and
grow like a plant,
absorbing the small
infinite details of the landscape,
a dog, untethered,
bounding past,

two boys late for dinner
showing off on bicycles,
darkness,
cupped hands, someone stops
to light a cigarette beneath the trees,
and from the stillness of birds and leaves emerges
the extinct photogenic face
of the last of a tribe.
Moonrise.

Walking barefoot near the tideline, tossing sticks
for the waves to chase and fetch.
Opening one's mouth – it's perilous!

Well. That's it then. All beach grass has been withering since
Socrates, or looks it. Tide-shunning birds run up and down the
          sand,
the water, restless as it is, and curiously indivisible.

Sit down then. Rest your feet.
They're angular, sad,
mute. Little fourteenth-century portraits of the saints.

Walking, after rain. A haze
of insects over the fallen ponds.
Those failing apple trees that guard the edge of some
long-gone farm, do you remember? – the flowering branch
you pulled down for me, off-handed,
and from nowhere a raccoon, huge and comic, appeared,
blocking the path – everyone
standing their ground a moment, and then you
looked and shrugged, spoke to it in that way you have,
Hey, man, and it wandered away.
The petals had been flying in the fields. We
came across a paved road and the path ended,
the animals that made it could vanish...Our friend Steve,
all the summer past, had been gathering wildflower seeds, four
tons, reseeding the prairie – your hand among the
petals though, the same one that explains
away everything when you're down and drunk.
You'd been drinking out of boredom,
you even danced on the tables for us,
but all as a diversion, to lead us away
from the true disruption, that feelings aren't finite.
They vanish and recur, circuitous, like paths
one wanders on or loses, following the fields.

One summer, at the edge of an ordinary neighbourhood, a middle-aged woman kept a tortoise tied by a long red ribbon to a lime tree. Days and nights passed. It was clear, even as she stooped to offer bits of lettuce, frilly ends of vegetables, that she would rather have had one of those prehistoric horses no more than fourteen inches high, whose neighing one can now only imagine. To hear it gallop across the hardwood floor: a sound as delicate as the careless thrumming of fingers on a table-top, as she rapped her breakfast egg with the edge of a spoon. To make a bed of straw for it in a cut-down soft-drink carton in the basement. She might even have pictured a miniature stable beneath the workbench where the portable lathe stood ready for her husband's weekend excursions into the decorous frivolities of wooden chair legs without chairs, table legs devoid of tables.

Perhaps as penance for out-surviving its equine contemporary, the tortoise had to live outdoors, on its own. It would not have made a distinction between indoors and outdoors in any case, and it was, with its lipless smile, a master of the art of doing penance. One day, we children, looking without success to play with it, were forced at last to admit that it was gone. Escaped, no doubt, from that world of obscure and immutable rules, into the hills, trailing its red ribbon, of which, though we ran about and strained to see, we could find no trace in the tall burgeoning straw.

Blackness and trees.
Heading south.
Blue fog from warehouse windows.
Highway 27.
A few night travellers.
Brushing glowing feelers as we pass.
29 November.
This 87th year of the century.
Yes.
Having done away with greatness.

Woken from somewhere. Woken from what was about to happen and now never will. Hear the rain. Tickling the innermost leaves. Watching with eyes closed, can see Kim moving around by the sounds. Everything memorized. A football game tumbling silent across the screen while he cooks, Kim at 5'11", the players 9 inches high tripping over each other in the replays like spiralling snow. Kim in a kind of hibernation. Pink pearly rabbit, skinned from head to toe, frying in the pan.

The improvisation is to lie exactly where I am and listen as if composing it myself, moment by moment. That winding private story I followed so intently while I dozed: no loss to wake up from it. The rain, just now, was playing a piece I wanted to hear. Singling out the notes, the hollow drumming spaces. Black miles of mud. Skeletal blades and handles washed up between the rows. Stiff ruffled lettuce, the last of the year, the regal bearing of a snail propelling it up and down the lopsided stalks like the ghost of a dead queen. A few pumpkins, freed from their vines. And pale green cabbages, rain streaming down the swollen veins. Cabbages, lying wide awake in the fields.

Rising unperturbed from the
rubble of the construction site,
you take us by surprise,
above the blocky angles of a city hospital,
over swamps, villages in foreign countries
where we've felt foreign,
unable even to ask for an apple or a toilet,
or at the head of Vulcan Stairway
in the San Francisco night
made wise by you,
and the knowing flowers
which stand like death masks.
In the least probable places you appear,
simultaneous,
everywhere at home,
everywhere equal.
Bright nude, round and full as a Reubens,
I've seen you recline even as you were borne up.
You demonstrate the false science of levitation.
Or, inert, a wan
sliver, aloft in pale blue, lost in our days,
while we think only of our own effort,
our clocks, our meals...
That you move
not by degree, as we do,
not in steps, or by leaping,
but in one long frictionless
departure, a constancy
as irksome as a tapping foot,
and this alien calm
would drive us mad –
What of other moons?
Do they fall as you fall,
like the white petals

of the spring apricot,
like a discus,
or the end of romantic love
as seen from tedious, lifeless planets?
Why is it that you look so far away
when only hours ago you
burst into our rooms and silences –
and we felt our humanity,
the conspiracy of our being.

How many hundreds of miles until it feels like standing still – and yet at the motel the sense of motion never ceases. The room with its crude painting over the bed, suffused, like an icon, with the glances of countless persons. One after another we move through this life, crowding the one ahead of us. And how he curls around me, eyes closed, a hand on my breast. As though the sum total of human knowledge were there, while we sleep.

I watched the breathing,
watched it die down,
the way, as a child,
I watched
the music box,
and how the key would
stop and then move on,
in little jerks,
fragmented,
I would have to strain
to recognize the tune.
It was a silly song.
About a goat, I think,
and someone standing, waiting,
on a hill.

Rushes of silver light. A little wind plays by itself in the corner of the plaza with whatever: lost leaves, bits of wrapper. Tall shocks of light from the buildings which are only mirrors trying to come clear. A gull, squawking, dips around the Royal Bank tower. Here and there the bombed-out look of bare structure, steel waiting for glass. Only the clues. A pair of trousers stuffed into a hedge, no explanation. A single shoe overturned on Yonge Street, passed back and forth all night by the wheels of opposing cars, now left alone in the morning light, pointing north.

North along the clean dirt road that led us one day to a meadow, unfindable again, dyed cherry-colour by the fallen sun, our shadows dark red, matching the blood inside. A few birds trickled from tree to tree, lost bits of a waterfall. Tunnelling worms that know nothing and see nothing, in those bare apples left to the branches. A queer country darkness came down around us. Hidden creatures turning up their volume, the fields on either side of the road competing in opposing keys. The lens of the earth's gases, before which we sat in the meadow, myopic, watching the stars flicker like movie screens in a far-off future. Given the chance you'd take a one-way trip there over the rest of your life on earth, you said. How beautiful, I thought, glancing over at Toronto. To inhabit that plane of lights intersecting nothing.

These are the roads you can drive without maps. And get there, nearly anywhere and back, without knowing, in between, where you've been. Concession roads and county roads criss-cross in a straight warp and woof so that it is possible to traverse a diagonal by merely turning right, left, and right again, every few miles. Navigating by whim. Signs for Cheltenham, Belfountain. Kidnapped to sudden unlikely gorges, rocky and treed with maples, birches that have spent all summer concentrating sunlight in their leaves – then back to acres of corn in tatters. Here and there the gnome-like figure of an apple tree, attended by birds. Apples still green on the branches, or fallen beneath them, deflating. As on a mirror in which autumn is the corrupted image of summer.

His father had spotted them first. Wild grapes,
high in the branches of a dead elm
in the empty lot next door.
Old friends, we were outside Santa Rosa,
visiting parents, a day in the country. *Swaying,*

in too-large borrowed boots,
unsteadied by the ladder –
but we got it leaned against the trunk,
the legs of the v straddling
a concealed stream meshed with brambles,
then saw, all around, at head height,
straggly clusters,
and gorged on these.
We were childhood lovers again,
I no more than thirteen, he
intent and restless, toppling blue-black grapes
into five-gallon buckets. The grapes were just past prime,
a little musty. Then he climbed the ladder.

Afterwards, when we'd hauled them all to the garage,
slipped off the muddy boots
and returned in our own shoes to the house,
his younger brother, who'd been unwell,
tasted some and nearly spat them out.
Lately he had wanted nothing but to sleep.
His illness was of the appetite,
of desire – and when I'd known him last
he'd been just a kid, and I
preoccupied with romance and his older brother.
After that orgy of scavenging, *so life is*
endless then, befriended,
in love with the past and a whole family,
I asked him to go walking,

to prod him, keep him awake.
And we did,
each choosing the unknown fork.
Wandering, really.
Along darkening local roads.

Last fall at Walter's farm, we all chopped wood and hauled it, John manning the tractor, hat cocked, brow lifted in one of those innocent stool-pigeon looks. The gentle bull spouting gentle bull. Afterwards we stood around and sweated, while for seconds on end not one leaf fell. Then we drifted in for beer, time for the game to start, while, down the field of milky light studded with the brown burst pods of milkweed, Paul and Roman strolled, solemn and private, I could see their mouths move – as though we, the day, the wood, were a proposition to be argued, hands in pockets, each half-turned from the other, from us, the blue of the bay.

The moon
like a knife.
The bay, breathing,
the town asleep along the shore
except for the elongated shriek
of a Chevy at the outskirts laying a
strip a mile long,
somebody's signature.
Clear nights and the moon looks down,
even in a town with nothing to do.
And the fifteen-year-old boys will think of something,
drinking or cars, they'll find a way
to compress that daring,
just a little, wandering the fields at
midnight, boozy, urinating into the fallen fruit,
the hard wild pears
of land long since abandoned.
The urine makes a faint
sizzling sound.
Only a few stray cattle,
looking up, erasing the grass from the fields,
as if each one weighed a ton
and the whole ton ached.
And then they're gone,
the teenaged boys,
the rocks thrown through the window frame
of the lost cabin, its huge mossy beams
collapsed in a criss-cross of moonlight,
and where the door would once have been
once more a pair of lilacs
that flicker and blow out,
spring upon winter,
year by year.
The town is asleep.

And because of it, the hour,
which hangs complete,
suspended,
like a bitter ripened fruit.

Chameleon evenings,
and a walking stick to poke down
under leaf mold,
go tapping the slow
wooden xylophone of trunks.
Forest, pasture, orchards
nearly weightless, without song.
And on, and on,
to the spongy heart of the field,
where the spring wells up:
to pause awhile, having travelled
miles, years.

The pond has frozen over, where in summer
a pig turned on the spit like something out of
Lord Of The Flies, and Steve, on his hands and knees,
grazed on tiny strawberries,
while woolly-headed John
snoozed like a sheepdog in the sun.
Now we're foraging for more wood.
Cameron, sleeves rolled,
tinkers with slivers and flame
like a boy building an airplane out of toothpicks.
Shoo the smoke out, shut the door, and we're in,
no talking now, just breathing.
Richard goes to saw a hole in the ice.
This is before fatherhood and various deaths,
before we all gave up
one future after another,
or succumbed, or got serious,
and defeat came into our lives.
John in his huge solid body, shy David
in his underwear, Cameron who moves like a whippet.
Air so hot it singes the nostrils,
and that water under ice, to which John says
No way but comes back grinning.
All afternoon we're taking turns,
lowered past the brain,
pulled out by the elbows –
and I'm running back,
past years and children,
suicide,
careers,
to steam and nakedness,
to close companionable sweat.
Running back.
To blue sky. Heat. Beautiful Richard of the ice saw.

Between night and morning the freshened airy streets lie quiet. All night the spasms of rain and thunder and the calm that follows. What is it summer will finally give birth to? At this hour I walk invisibly, protected and alone, following a faint scent of angel that precedes me through the streets. And here before your darkened house: one starry light left on to say you will return this time, that you are only far away in a city I have not seen.

Before dawn I climb to your back porch where the morning glories dangle dripping wires, like downed phone lines, in the exaggerated quiet after storm. The flowers are sleeping, bright and twisted, hooked through the matted vine, each a day of summer still to come. Yesterday's are puckered, tobacco-coloured, as if life passed through them too quickly, barely rippling the surface.

These morning glories. Blue summer thunder.

I can no longer account for the dark heart-shaped leaves that hang between us, wherever we are now. It has always been that when we looked at one another we saw clearly some thing that should be passed down, as among brothers, an inheritance. But we are awkward with our differences – man, woman, these small things. Possibly you are only asleep even now, a sleep you will walk out of as from a city whose ruin I have not witnessed, to catch me stealing time with your morning glories. They are like children, taunting us for having limits.

Stubborn as a mule, the saying goes,
or that friendship has long ears, and can be speechless.
I'm thinking of that dinner party, one of the last
of a certain era. Helping to carry chairs out
to the balcony, hunting for more, deep in the apartment,
as our women friends arrived amid the bustle of drinks, and it
          took
five of us just to manoeuvre the table out. The meal then,
fine Greek bread from the corner bakery, the stories
passed around with the wine, awkward, humorous, ironic, of
beds and those early boyfriends, everyone's first fall.
Maybe it was partial amnesia,
or that I wasn't directly asked – shyness,
loyalty to the boy, not knowing how to tell it without
betraying its small intimacies – whatever – and
then the conversation moved on. Up there
on the balcony, among summer trees,
I suppose we *were* loud, and that the woman next door
had a right to complain: we didn't know
anyone had to sleep, ever,
or get up in the morning. Leaving the past and the plates
          though,
moving indoors, it struck me, Mary,
how for months I'd been paralyzed in some way,
like looking in a mirror, flustered at seeing you in that pain.
I wanted to put words to it, bring you out the other side.
That the myth of the goddess and the myth of the monster
are one, that a love half loathing isn't love
but infidelity and narcissism...
But friends are no jury for lovers, and words
are too easily awkward, and make
bad models. Susan said it best.

Her hands, as usual, composing the fruit bowl,
a rendering both beautiful and edible, without any question
of how much to give or withold.
Just giving what there is.
Love, Roo.

Through the hilly streets
musty with late rain and rich houses,
in his black leather jacket,
a second skin if cats have nine,
he motorcycles off,
leaving us chilly
atop Indian Rock.

All afternoon my brother Ben
has been spidering about,
pulling himself up on unseen threads,
doing "The Chute" and "Borson's Folly,"
a climb he devised.
He knows every handhold on the rock,
is still picking new routes over the face.

On his new bike
Steve did seventy, recently,
up Marin,
flew over the intersection.

What I love
is not the rock
or the speed
but how they depend on them,
on certain calculations.

The central star in Orion's
sword: how it's taken since before the birth of Christ
for tonight's light to reach us.

Today, Tracy, it came back to me,
the letter you sent, years ago now. How it arrived,
forwarded and reforwarded, out of the blue –
one for each of us, I thought then, the old high school crowd,
hoping to find out what everyone was up to.
It started me poking through drawers, old boxes,
the letter itself set aside for the moment.
Books, brassieres, boys – no more than a couple of years, really,
and still, you wrote, *we appear in dreams or*
cross paths somehow, and things
get connected over time.
I'd been thinking
about last summer just before that, Suzanne and I
driving off from her parents' house. I can still see her,
the hand on the wheel, so tight the knuckles were white
            from it,
and she, not even noticing, just getting the hell
out of Stockton, but also
there was that larger, untenable urge,
to turn back, not leave them there,
though it was the life they had made.
The darkening almond groves were already behind us,
we were passing through Tracy
when your name and the letter came back to me.
A few miles on we had a flat. Now that
was a surprise, we'd neither of us
changed a tire before. To walk
the unlit freeway to the lights of the next small town
or flag down some man in a passing car and be saved –
it never occurred to us to trust ourselves or logic,
and I've been remembering
how fresh the night had seemed, that irreverent,
random element; that when we were finally on our way again
we had to stop: Suzanne, shaken,

a few people in a small-town café, the glass of milk in her hand.
Thinking too of your letter,
the sudden need to connect.
I looked for it tonight.
Gone, lost in the layers.
And of Suzanne, two thousand miles away. Confused,
just now, imagining I could pick out
among the lights of the city
the dark of her apartment.
A little sorry I've moved on.

Across the blue-grey radius of industry and blurred lake water,
neighbourhoods camouflaged by trees,
past the plaster well in the lawn which gathers, now and then,
a little rain for the pronged feet of a bird to splash in,
past the hand-painted plaster saint who guards
the tender summer yard as though journeying forever across
        water,
and the moon just up, like
someone stumbled out of bed, one cheek unevenly shaven,
the grapes in real clusters on the trellis –
and even as she sleeps, the girl's body
being shaped there, subtly, over time, like a guitar
the grown men long to play again.

After a long night the first objects spring out, dazed. The table-top, a cup with a little left in it. All night between memories and this instant I've been tossed like a ball for the amusement and betrayal of the beautiful shepherd, Prince, who watches from his corner with sad unmistaken eyes, wanting nothing more than to play this game with me. Dog I cannot possibly remember, dog I know only through stories and Kim's eyes: eyes out of which, unbeckoned, Prince would bound, or stand dancing, mouth wide – and old pains too, the back legs, crippled before he died. He'd like to shake the memories from me like moths from an old coat, as if memories were a grudge I hold against this present life. And how can I deny them? Eyes out of which Prince comes bounding, pure trust, through daylight meadows blue and fragile with invented games.

There were predecessors.
Little Poo, who ran from mice,
assasinated at seventeen
by a city councilman's dog.
Rover, or Tiger,
Shalmonizar, depending on his mood,
who trod the garden paths
and uttered my name.
Neurotic Peachbottom,
the grey beauty,
whom a blind finger named,
touching down on the atlas
at a Pennsylvania town.
And the brothers,
one the runt and one the giant,
Paddy, who escaped the
vet's knife, fought, and died
under the house,
and Toby, long-legged, courteous,
clean-cut connoisseur of baseball,
eunuch,
who lived on to drool on girls
and chew their hair.
There are, too,
those I know only as legends,
imbibers of watermelon,
nibblers of spaghetti,
furtive pee-ers
in the shoes of overnight guests.
To these let me add
this one,
orphan, homebody, dispatcher of shrews,
discovered later, mummificant,
right-angular, in the corners of rooms,

dandler of scorpions,
scholar of roses,
lover of caramelized
Norwegian cheese.
This one,
known in his time as all of these.
Proud trapper of pens and string,
of mice, by his own genius,
in long-forgotten Roach Motels beneath the sink.
The lonely feel of ankles now.
A long-shed claw at the foot of the bed.
Those strands of fur which cling,
the separate threads of stripedness,
to everything.

On television, two giant leopard slugs
flow up a trunk
and then dangle together
from a rope of their own slime.
A pale fungal cloud,
the mating organ, emerges
from the side of each head –
When it is done,
one falls to the ground,
and the other returns, painstakingly,
the way they had come.
All of this is usual.
A garden snail,
waylaid by an albino
of another species, a meat-eater,
wrestles for its life and loses,
trying to escape from its shell.

With television, what one of us sees,
we all see.
In the dark, just outside,
they climb the vines,
sucking the skin
from the tomatoes, leaving raw
unhealing patches.
By morning they'll be gone.
Once we went out with a flashlight.
Flung the snails down,
breaking their shells.
The slugs we teased off with a stick and salted,
so they writhed and shrank.

In The Wizard Of Oz,
in the early days of colour,

Dorothy stands back like that too.
A horror so stylized
it's almost delight.
Stands back,
in this world which is neither home nor Kansas,
while the Wicked Witch of the West
howls, melts.

Around the houses for miles, in a century
of usual delusions, history – this waterfall of rain.
All afternoon the two of us,
during, after, for.
Spreading through the breasts,
the uterus, the parts of the body that have to do
with giving up, giving over to the
new – no shame. Such afternoons are few.
It would be sweet to begin again,
as the rain starts up, never failing to surprise.
Those who've never cried from happiness,
these are allowed to love the rain.

Seeing that there's no other way,
I turn his absence into a chair.
I can sit in it,
gaze out through the window.
I can do what I do best
and then go out into the world.
And I can return then with my useless love,
to rest,
because the chair is there.

Sunflowers' thick stems twisted over, wild yellow curls around the heavy heads, and paired leaves hunched behind like the shoulder-blades of "The Thinker," those poised scales that weigh one thing against another, weigh bronze against air and find them equal, though never balancing. The sunflowers stoop toward summer's end. Nearby, sunrays burn in and out of the copper eyes of a frog, hanging stiff as a little drowned man in the water. Kim, as on all other afternoons, bent over a problem, something with equations, which he spreads across the page, looking between them for the lost error. His shoulders still balancing one thing against another. He loves me. Life will not last.

On the far side of the house two cats roll in sunshine in the catnip patch – they would roll there forever if catnip didn't work its hazy forgetful pleasures – and then they stalk off, stiff-legged, drunkards. Not a yard away, in shadow, the weeds sprout their ragged hearts. The dark part of the garden, left to go to seed – smoky moth, spider in a gauzy net. The place everyone's eye passes over as it makes its rounds. The blind spot. Where everything we do not care to look at lives.

Nighttime, summer countryside. Insects sticking like magnets to the lit screens of the house. In the dark garden it's like standing at the weedy bottom of a well, staring straight up. Kim's shoulders with that athletic tension in them that never gives out. Not just some. All the stars.

After ten afternoons Kim has found the error and moved on, engrossed again. Boxcars of an almost endless train in the distance, metal grumbling about being next to metal. Beyond the mown fields, web of trees, down along the railbed the grey, glinty-eyed rocks, full of frozen forms. Faint moon, exactly torn in half.

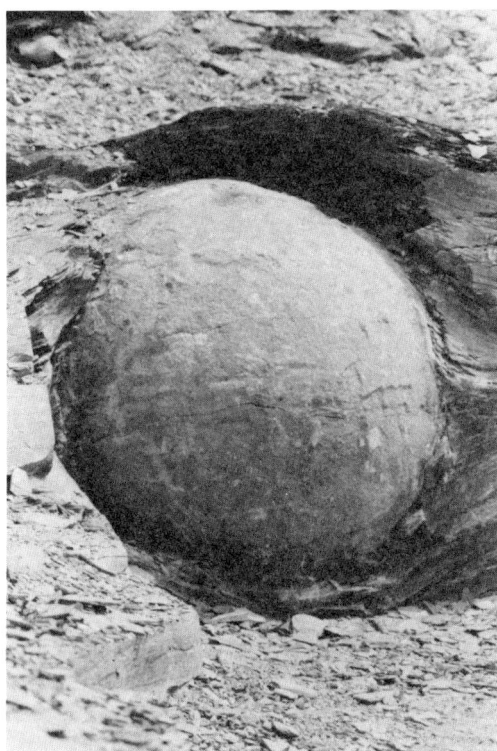

Save us from night,
from bleak open highways
without end, and the fluorescent
oases of gas stations,
from the gunning of immortal
engines past midnight,
when time has no meaning,
from all-night cafés,
their ghoulish slices of pie,
and the orange ruffle on the
apron of the waitress,
the matching plastic chairs,
from orange and brown and
all unearthly colours,
banish them back to the test tube,
save us from them,
from those bathrooms with a
moonscape of skin in the mirror,
from fatigue, its merciless brightness,
when each cell of the body stands on end,
and the sensation of teeth,
and the mind's eternal sentry,
and the unmapped city
with its cold bed.
Save us from insomnia,
its treadmill,
its school bells and factory bells,
from living-rooms like the tomb,
their plaid chesterfields
and galaxies of dust,
from chairs without arms,
from any matched set of furniture,
from floor-length drapes which
close out the world,

from padded bras and rented suits,
from any object in which horror is concealed.
Save us from waking after nightmares,
save us from nightmares,
from other worlds,
from the mute, immobile contours
of dressers and shoes,
from another measureless day, save us.

And still I walk here,
and think of you, things not
as they were –
but that's the way it is, of course.
That I can no longer remember
which building you lived in,
the window you'd peer out from
and then go strolling with Anne...
That you chose
never to hear, or feel, anymore.
And I keep seeing you float up,
long past winter and the thaw,
to be found, finally; keep seeing
that indolent, impassive squint as you'd
light a cigarette: the far distance.
And yet you loved it here,
in the thick of summer, couples
lolling as if hidden by the short grass,
martyred to the kiss:
they roll, first one way,
then another, the leaves: October.
Had you cared for anything again,
it would have been to have walked here,
and known this.
And so I place you,
in memory, silently smoking.
Skittish migrations of leaves across the lawns.
Drunks, rolled in old coats,
claiming the full length of the benches.
Snow soon.

Past midnight I sink my head into the feather pillow. At last! We are all solitary travellers. The motel lights have dimmed. A key in another door: someone letting himself in, at any hour. Just alongside my right ear, or beside the night table with its standing glass of water, or just outside the sliding glass door, loud and wide in the dark, the river, fed by mountains, without beginning or end, knowing not its own name, or lore, or the name of the town, or my name.

The grapes were wild, frosted purple in a sunset giving way to dusk. When the moon sat on its ledge above the fields it painted glossy windows on those bunches where a fox had brushed past, or a jackrabbit, rubbing off that bit of blue mist. If you ran a comb through these fields you'd come up with a natural history of the region. Foxes and jackrabbits. The sails and rigging of bodies finally too ungovernable to navigate this last stormy passage, this hollow of combat in the smoothed straw. Under the moon of poor eyesight, the moon which sees everything in the faded shades of an old colour photograph, these bones become the abstract artifacts of movement and ruin. The shields, the sails of the pelvis. The masts, and columns. This is the wilderness we came to: feuds nursed slowly over centuries, minuets of violence in the blonde fields, the hautiness with which one animal sees another, as if a lens had been inserted into the eye. The etiquette of such a death.

Grapes grew wild across North America – black grapes with iridescent flesh. Through the dark froth of bushes, tall, stately, a stag appears, a ghost ship.

Then it can begin.
Like a little girl urinating for the first time in the open,
the rain, the shy rain,
hearing herself,
begin.
Or the woman remembering this.
And you beside me, sleeping,
in the burning desert of the reading lamp.

It is a matter of spaces. Of infinitesimal nutrients built up over time. Of constant sound, as of hinges or newborn beings. How pleasant it is to be lost among the powerful sunlit columns. Nothing is obscured except by grandeur, nothing concealed. Pleasant, that is, unless you stray too long and dusk begins, which fills the legs with sand. Yet if you can stand just a little indiscriminate terror, if you can endure not knowing (never to know) whether you are being honoured on this earth or not so much as marked in passing: either way. And it will reveal itself, the alien, tribal nature of the grove. Stars called into being above the swaying crowns.

Their lives are longer, slower than ours.
They drink more deeply, slowly,
are warmed, do not shiver at dusk.
The heart unwinding makes a small noise.
Who would hear it?
Yet the trees attend,
perhaps to us, perhaps to nothing,
fragrance maybe, not of
flowering, but leaves and bark.
Trees. Dusk. Hand-coloured photographs
of the world before we were born.
Not sweet, but as water is,
sweet to a mouth long closed on itself.
Befriend them.

It was two nights after our father's death,
and we lay against the hill,
slowly passing the binoculars.

I'd been drinking coffee,
thinking about my mother's long silver hair.

Whenever I'm idle I remember how it was.

I'm standing on the muscled
rock sloping down to the water,

rock like the petrified
haunches of mammals,
marbled, sedimentary,

as if, in rugged prehistory
with its abstract cataclysms,
behemoths, mammoths
tumbled here to extinction.

The idea
that nothing actually leaves the earth
I misunderstood profoundly,
at an age when I had barely
grasped my own name,
following my mother over the rocks.

Taken literally,
it becomes a kind of myth,
uncorrected at its depths,
beckoning,

so that even now,
when I come upon such a cove,
in the escalating roar
and the transformed rocks,

I see her, large-boned, moving ahead of me.

Late one night we listened, his gift, near the
end of love, just as there is a limit
to what the eye can count at a glance,
those few inextricable voices making
an infinitude, grief, celebration, the window beyond which
snow fell, bye love,
David's hand around my hand.

From here the city appears a chalky fortress, incandescent against thunder-bearing skies which admit, now and then, briefly, beams whose apparent purpose is to cauterize excessive beauty from the grass and then move on, though how one patch of grass differs from another is anyone's guess. This weather holds the subtle power of an egg, or seed, a hand stayed in anger, an inscrutable intent before which all rays and beams, all special effects, seem child's play, or else half bluff, like the courting gestures of the peacock or the newt – the antics of my two grown male friends, for instance, who cavort across the grass – shouts of *Isadora Duncan! Isadora Duncan!* – stripped of shirts, manners, career, all loves but a clandestine love for being unwilled in the sudden larger universe. Against such skies the cottonwoods grow ponderous, the willows barely breathing. No more to bend in an attitude of solitude. No more to serve as objects of yearning! Like them we're free to be misled utterly, to continue on our chosen path, as if forever, without hindrance...to stroll among the darkening office towers and condominiums across the water, where manners, career, shirts in the morning all unfold – and remark, of nothing in particular, like passersby before yet another of those perpetually unfinished public buildings, "Yes, but what's it for?" or "I'll bet that's costing the taxpayers a pretty penny!"

If you sit still long enough doing nothing, even the birds will forgive your presence. A paddling mallard in a skirt of froth, that unfathomable expression full of fish about it. And the shy, hypnotized fliers, fluctuating out of nowhere, behind trees.

Those trees whose shade we sat in all afternoon, dreaming up theories. A theory of clouds! A theory of grass blades. Voices of friends at a distance now, elastic on the evening air. The frisbee hovers for a moment and then falls.

Beside the sliding surf, a blue crab claw, fired orange at the joints, perfectly empty on the sand, cream-coloured on the under (private) side, still casts its shadow. Things that have lived have this light in them.

And then approaches the last ferry, our antics die down, and we wait quietly, if a little reluctantly, but tired and ready, for we are not perpetual motion machines, as the ferry glides in for that random thud, wood against wood, the signal that we can board. Or we could board, except for the uniformed gentleman who, every twenty minutes, back and forth from the mainland, holds departing and prospective passengers at bay, with great ceremony, and finally, at his pleasure, unhooks the rope.

Engine, captain, lifebuoys aside, the essence of the ferry is wood, which floats upon water, and whose varnished grain, in the last rays, gives off such homesickness. Homesickness for the forest, for that primeval state which we have just shaken off so that we might return to the city, to a life in which each transaction must be earned and paid for.

The brief return trip is thus imbued with the momentousness of our voluntary parting from what we think of so fondly as our true nature; a willful sacrifice, an anguish indistinguishable from the ease of coming back to familiar life. At sundown another ship drifts nearby. Music comes from it, and soon there will be dancing. The ship is tiered, lit up like the birthday cake of a prince or a queen as seen from childhood, a childhood in which only what was codified seemed beautiful. For back then we had to build everything up from nothing, ignorant of the means, that the goal might be merely to reach these very moments in which we flirt with the impulse to demolish all. That foolish notion of courage. And yet finally our image of happiness is complete, insatiable! To live it all again, but this time with full consciousness, *saturated* with consciousness.

About the Cat, 92
Adjustments to the Hair and
    Clothes, 4
After a Death, 97
After Argument, 63
Afternoon Nap, Dark Day, 67
Afternoon Rain, 96
Allan Gardens, 103
And, 14
Autumn, 29
Autumn Incidents, 34
Backroads, 76
Carmel by the Sea, 38
Chitons, 7
City, 75
City Lights, 55
Clear Nights, 80
Close to the Beginning, 110
Coming into Summer, 3
Dawn in the Massif Central, 24
Digging Song, 47
False Spring, 48
Fields for John Martin, 64
Final Landscape, 37
Finding Halley's Comet, 109
Fingernails, 52
From the Island, 112
Grief, 32
Grove, 107
Here, 60
Highway 27, 66
Hockey Night in Canada, 58
House, 10
Indian Rock: Afternoon, Evening,
    87
Intent, or the Weight of the
    World, 39
Intermittent Rain, 16
Jogging, 53

Laboured Breathing, 71
Late Autumn Walking Song, 82
Leaving the Island, 114
Lust, 1
Moon, 68
Morning Glories, for N., 84
Near Cannington, 9
Nebraska, 70
On the Island, 113
Pine, 33
Poem Beginning with a Line by
    Anne Michaels, 31
Ranjan's Horse, 59
Remembering Early Bach, As It
    Was Given, 111
Robert Pinsky Was Standing on
    the Corner in a Black Leather
    Jacket with His Face Screwed
    Up into a Moue, 49
Rubber Boots, 5
Sauna, Hart House Farm, 83
Save Us from, 101
Small Pains, 20
Small Song, 51
Snowlight on the Northwood
    Path, 11
Some Thoughts, and a Letter, 85
Spiders and Snails, 57
Spring Poem, 61
Spring's Fever, 36
Subtle Music, 90
Sympathetic Magic, 91
The Gift, for Robert Bringhurst, 28
The Irony, 27
The Limits of Knowledge, Tilton
    School, New Hampshire, 22
The Merchants' Song, 30
The Thinker, Stone Orchard, 98
The Trees, 108

Time Alone, 50
Toronto, 18
Tortoise, 65
Tracy, 88
Travelling, 104
2 A.M., 13
Two Horses, 35
Ways of Being, Georgian Bay, 79
We're Out with the Night Beings,
    21
Wild Grapes, 77
Wild Grapes, America, 105
Wild World, 94
Working and Getting to Sleep on
    Time, 106

A NOTE ON THE TEXT

A number of people and institutions have helped bring this book into being. I would like to thank Kim Maltman for all of his work on all of my work; Don McKay and Jan Zwicky for the use of their eyes and ears; Andy Patton for the cover painting; Sue Schenk and Steve Schwartz for the photos; the Canada Council, the Ontario Arts Council, and the N.E.A. for their support at various times over the last several years; and the following journals and anthologies for first publishing the poems: *Anything Is Possible; Canadian Fiction Magazine; The Canadian Forum; Cutbank; Dandelion; Deep Down, The New Sensual Writing By Women; Fireweed; Four By Four; NeWest Review; Poetry Australia; Poetry Canada Review; Rubicon; Saturday Night; The Greenfield Review; The Lyric Paragraph; The Malahat Review; The New Quarterly; This Magazine; Toronto Life; West Coast Review; Western Living*.

Some books are journeys; this is a room with windows. If there is any organizing principle (for here one may come and go as one pleases), or any point to be taken, it is to preserve the dark in the light and the light in the dark. As I said to a friend recently, this is a collection of whatever's been on my mind the last few years. All except for the recipes, jokes, and grocery lists, and that which still hasn't found a way into words.

This book is for Kim.